TIME OUT!

DEVOTIONS FOR ATHLETES

J. PATRICK STREET

TIME OUT

J. Patrick Street, Time Out

ISBN 1-929478-17-8

Cross Training Publishing
317 West Second Street
Grand Island, NE 68801
(308) 384-5762

This book is manufactured in the United States of America.

Library of Congress Cataloging in Publication Data in Progress.

Published by Cross Training Publishing,
317 West Second Street
Grand Island, NE 68801
1-800-430-8588
www.crosstrainingpublishing.com

I dedicate this book
to my parents, John and Estella Street,
for their love, encouragement, and
continual challenge to do my best.

CONTENTS

COACHING TIP

First, fixing your habit concerning a quiet time will bring you a quiet heart, a quiet confidence and a quiet power.

THE EFFECTIVE QUIET TIME

To be spiritually contagious, we must provide for replenishing our inner resources. This is done in the **quiet time**. The quiet time shuts you in with the Lord to experience His presence, His peace, and His power, that you might be lifted to a higher level.

You can't maintain a spiritually contagious life unless you take a specific time daily for prayer and Bible study. It will fade out. So take the following steps:

(1) **Decide on a time** you can give as a quiet time before the Lord, preferably in the morning. It tunes your heart for the day.

"My voice shalt thou hear in the morning, O Lord; in the morning will I direct my prayer unto thee, and will look up" (Psalm 5:3).

(2) Having fixed a time, **stick to it**. Pray, whether you feel like it or not.

(3) **Read your Bible.** Let it soak in. It will release new meaning to you. In a notebook, write down what you hear God saying to you as you read.

(4) Next, **relax and listen**, become guidable. Remember, prayer is a dialogue, not a monologue.

(5) **Thank the Lord** for the answers. Praising God is a great way to give thanks. We worship the Lord for who He is, but we praise the Lord for what He has done, is doing, and will do.

"Seven times a day do I praise thee because of thy righteous judgements" (Psalm 119:164).

(6) **Use these devotions as a starting point.** Look up the suggested scripture passages, and reflect

on their meaning. Try to incorporate some of the suggestions into your daily life.

STEPS TOWARD A REAL PRAYER LIFE

The disciples asked Jesus to share His secret concerning prayer: "Lord, teach us to pray" (Luke 11:1). He answered by teaching them the Lord's prayer (Luke 11:2-4):

"Our Father, which art in heaven, hallowed be thy Name; Thy kingdom come, Thy will be done, on Earth, as it is in heaven. Give us this day our daily bread, and forgive us our sins, as we forgive those who sin against us; and lead us not into temptation, but deliver us from evil, for Thine is the kingdom, and the power, and the glory forever, amen."

The prayer can be divided into two parts: (1) the God-side: "our Father, Thy name, Thy kingdom, Thy will." (2) the human-side: "give us, forgive us, lead us, deliver us." The first side is "realignment" and the second side is "result." In the first side we realign (ally ourselves) to our Father, to His name, to His kingdom, to His will, and in the second, we get the result--He gives to us, forgives us, leads us, and delivers us. In other words, we get as much "result" as we have "realignment." The emphasis, then, should be on the realignment, and the result will take care of itself.

The following are six practical steps to help establish a real prayer life:

(1) Determine that a vital prayer life is the most important factor in your life with the Lord. To be God-possessed we must be prayer-possessed.

(2) Remind yourself that God is more anxious than you to set up a relationship of two-way prayer. We do not have to overcome God's reluctance. We can rely on His willingness to answer our prayers.

(3) Organize your day around your prayer time. Don't let the day decide your time of prayer. Fix a time and stay with it so that each day you don't have to debate the question.

(4) Believe that the Lord hears your prayers and will give you what you need, at the time needed. Not necessarily what you ask, but what you need. Believe it will be as good as you ask, or better.

(5) If your mind wanders, don't be discouraged. Pray for the thing to which your mind wandered. In this way you can redeem the wandering.

(6) If, in the course of your day, you have to wait for anybody or for anything, fill in that waiting time with prayer. This saves you from frustration and makes the waiting a victorious time.

COACHING TIP

Talk with God,
No breath is lost,
Talk On!

Walk with God,
No strength is lost,
Walk on!

Wait on God,
No time is lost,
Wait on!

THE "HOME RUN KING"

Babe Ruth was known far and wide as the "home run king" of baseball for many years because he hit 714 home runs during his great career. But the Babe was also the "strike-out king." He struck out 1,330 times, nearly twice as many times as he hit homers.

Ruth said he discovered a law of averages in his batting, that for every three times he struck out he was due two home runs.

Ruth's law of averages was put to the test in the last game of the season, which would decide the pennant. Lefty Grove was pitching for Philadelphia and Babe came to bat in the ninth inning, with two outs and the score tied. Ruth thought, Lefty has struck me out three times. I'm due my first home run.

Grove eyed home plate and threw two strikes and three balls. With the count full, the crowd grew deathly still. With the next pitch a crack was heard, and everyone knew the ball was over the fence and Babe Ruth had won the game for the Yankees.

Sometimes, the world's evil tries to "strike you out," but you are on the winning team. Jesus has already won the game for you! If you fail or problems attack you, don't give up--the Lord's law of averages works for you too. Jesus said, "In the world you have tribulation, but take courage; I have overcome the world" (John 16:33).

THE FAST BALL

The batter stands at the plate, the ball is coming at him at the rate of 90 to 95 miles per hour. In a third of a second, he must size up the pitch and decide to swing or not.

It is no wonder baseball players fail to hit more often than they succeed. Even the best hitters in baseball hit safely only three or four times out of every ten at bat. Time after time they ground out, fly out, or strike out. They are great hitters because their averages are high.

It is true in the game of life. Life throws us tough problems, and often we have to make quick decisions. Many of us lose heart because we fail so many times. Here is where the great batters can help us. Although they fail more often than they hit, they always go to the plate with a determination to knock the ball over the fence.

Paul put it this way: "...let us not lose heart in doing good, for in due time we shall reap if we do not grow weary" (Galatians 6:9). If we meet our problems with a courageous heart and a spirit of determination, our averages will be high too.

GOLF BALLS WITH DIMPLES

At the end of his first golf game, a young man was distressed to find that many of his smooth golf balls were covered with indentations. The next time he played, he used some of these balls and some smooth ones. The "dimpled" balls hit their targets more often than those that were smooth.

At that time, all golf balls were smooth. One manufacturer heard of the man's experience and conducted some experiments. He found that if he put indentations in the balls, they did indeed work better than the smooth ones. He used the man's trouble to improve his product.

Romans 5:3 says we are to rejoice when we have problems. With the Lord's help we cannot only overcome our problems, we can use them to create something better.

COACHING TIP

When we have nothing left but the Lord, we discover that the Lord is enough.

OVERCOMING HURDLES

In the 1960 Olympics, Wilma Rudolph won three gold medals for track and field, but getting there wasn't easy. At the age of 4, she lost the use of her left leg due to scarlet fever. At age 7, she had to learn to walk again.

How can you and I grow through struggles and come through in victory? First, we can grow in faith. Struggles compel us to turn to the Lord, to fully depend on Him to help us. As we trust in Him, we will discover that He never lets us down (see Romans 8:28).

Second, we can grow in our relationship with the Lord. When we turn to Him, He answers our prayers. His care for us shows He loves us...like a parent loves a child (see 2 Peter 5:7).

Third, in struggles, we grow to know the Lord's power. We learn that He really is greater than our problems and that His grace is sufficient to carry us through even in our weakness (see 2 Corinthians 12:9-10).

OVERCOMING THE "I CAN'T'S"

History is filled with men and women who have said, "I can," and succeeded in spite of severe physical limitations (see Hebrews 11).

In spite of his deafness, Beethoven composed some of the world's greatest symphonies. In spite of his blindness, Milton wrote some of the world's most beautiful literature. In spite of his stuttering, Cervantes became a public speaker of remarkable power. And in spite of crippling infantile paralysis, Franklin D. Roosevelt became the 32nd President of the United States.

President Roosevelt wrote shortly before his death, "The only limit to our realization of tomorrow will be our doubts of today. Let us move forward with a strong and active faith."

All too often we let an "I can't" attitude keep us from reaching our greatest potential. But a strong and active faith in the Lord and ourselves can change our "I can't's" to "I can do all things through Christ who strengthens me" (Philippians 4:13).

No matter the task before you, if it is French class, Algebra or running the anchor leg of the 4 X 400, let your belief be strong and active. You can!

COACHING TIP

It's always too soon to quit.

INTEGRITY

What is this thing called integrity? The dictionary definitions include terms like complete, uncorrupted, blameless, honest, and consistent. In a biblical context, integrity can be defined as the consistency and honesty that characterize the person who wants to obey and please the Lord.

Integrity is the glue that holds together our private life and our public life. It keeps our actions and our words connected to the truth.

Integrity is demonstrated when:

* You mean what you say.
* You live the way you say you believe.
* You don't pretend to be someone you are not.
* You have motives that are pure and unhidden.
* You don't keep silent when you should speak up.
* You can be trusted to do what you promise.
* You don't misrepresent the facts.
* You don't teach others something that you will not do.

Integrity demands that we should have nothing to cover up. We should not try to fool God or anyone else.

DON'T UNDERESTIMATE YOUR POTENTIAL

In Helsinki, Finland, at the first World Championships of track-and-field, Mary Decker (now Slaney) reaches the pinnacle of her career. She defeats the mighty Soviets to capture the 1500 and the 3000, to be known thereafter as the Double Decker. She is named Sportswoman of the year by *Sports Illustrated* as an affirmation of her success.

The Bible emphasizes over and over that single individuals can make a difference. God blessed the world through Noah, Abraham, Moses, David, and countless other individuals. And, of course, it was through one Man, Jesus Christ, that we today can receive the greatest blessing of all, the gift of eternal life (see Romans 5:19).

Perhaps you think, "How can I possibly make a difference in this world?" It's so easy to underestimate your potential, to think you have no influence, no ability to change your world. But when you are living a life that is acceptable to God, you do make a difference. You make a difference in your home, in your school, in your community--with God, you can do great things.

COACHING TIP

Circumstances don't make a person, they reveal what a person's made of.

SPIRITUAL BATTLE

I once heard a comedian say that he had gone to a prize fight, and a hockey game broke out. Hockey is a tough and demanding sport. It is common to see the battles of temper exchanged on the ice but often the players wear so much padding that the fights do little damage.

Of all the players on the hockey team, I marvel at the goalie. Not only is the puck being fired at him, but he has to know how to use his pads and stick against the attack--and that takes skill.

The Bible is to the Christian what the pads and stick are to the hockey goalie. Here are some ideas to help you build your skill in encountering God's Word.

1. **Have your own Bible** so that you can underline verses that speak to you.

2. **Have a regular time for Bible study**. Find a time when you can read several chapters at one sitting. Starting the day with the Bible puts God's Word in your heart to guide and direct you.

3. **Memorize scriptures.** Jesus himself committed the Word to memory and used it to defeat the temptation of Satan (see Matthew 4:1-11).

God's promises are promises to you personally. Read them, believe them and claim them for your own. When you faithfully study the Word of God each day and commit it to memory, you will find the answer to every problem that may come your way.

COACHING TIP

If your Christianity is worth having, it should be worth sharing!

RUNNING THE BASES

The ultimate thrill for a baseball player is to see the ball he just hit sail out of the ballpark for a homer. When we ask Jesus into our lives, the feeling is the same. It is a feeling of freedom and exhilaration. We are free from the bondage and burden of sin; but like the ballplayer who hits the home run, we have some "bases" still to run in our Christian life.

The first base, in our Christian run for home, is **confession**. That is, a daily as well as an initial confession of our sins.

The second base is **consecration** which is becoming more like Jesus--loving and forgiving others as He has forgiven us.

Third base is **commission**--telling others about what the Lord has done for us through His Son and letting the difference it has made show in our daily lives.

Home plate is **continuation**--the transformation that will take place when we take on the glorified body Jesus promises us.

The home-run hitter can either run or walk the bases, but he has to touch them all to score. As Christians, we are not touching all the bases to be saved. Proverbs says, "The righteous runneth into (the Lord), and is safe" (Proverbs 18:10). We are already safe in Jesus, as our Savior. We are running the bases because we want to be like Him and are following His "play book"--the Bible.

TO DISNEYLAND

The following story was shared at football chapel. There was a man driving on the outskirts of a city when he noticed a hog crossing a busy street. He jumped out of his pickup and caught it. Then he flagged down a policeman and said to him, "I got this hog out of the street. What should I do with it?"

The policeman said, "Take it to the zoo."

So he put the hog in his pickup and left.

The next day the policeman saw the man drive by with the hog sitting in the front seat. He pulled him over and said, "I thought I told you to take that thing to the zoo."

"We went there yesterday," the man answered. "Today we're going to Disneyland."

When two people misunderstand each other, the best laid plans can go sour. Sometimes it takes a third party to analyze the situation and work things out.

The Bible contains God's instructions to us. We could easily misinterpret them, so the Lord has given us an "interpreter" to help us: the Holy Spirit. Jesus taught that the Spirit would "...guide you into all truth" (John 16:13). God's Holy Spirit helps us understand what the Bible says and gives us the power to do all that we know the Lord wants us to do.

BOUNDARIES OF FREEDOM

The playground of an elementary school in the heart of a big city was between the school building and a busy street. The kids knew what could happen if they were to forget about the cars rushing by and chase a ball into the street. Though they were free to play anywhere, they stayed close to the school building. Then one day a fence was put around the entire school and the kids began to play freely on the grounds. They felt safe anywhere within the boundaries of the fence.

Like a fence between the schoolyard and a busy street, the boundaries in God's Word help us to walk within God's ways and away from sin, which could defeat and destroy us and those we sin against.

It is this "limited" freedom that truly makes us safe and joyful (Proverbs 29:18). When we follow the instructions in God's Word, we need not fear hurting ourselves and others. The Lord's commandments keep us in the blessings of God and make our lives a blessing to all around us.

COACHING TIP

One mark of a well-fed Christian is a well-read Bible.

SUCCESS AND FAILURE

The difference between success and failure often is very small. In the 1982 NCAA tournament, Georgetown and North Carolina traded shot-for-shot and point-for-point for 40 minutes. With 15 seconds to go and Georgetown behind by only one point, the final play of the game was the difference between becoming the NCAA champions and finishing in second place.

If you chart a football game, you will find that out of 80 to 100 plays executed, five or six key plays make the difference on the outcome of the game. If the coaches knew which plays these would be, they would practice all week on those particular plays to be sure they were executed to perfection.

The bottom line is, God's Word tells us what makes the difference between success and failure in our lives: "Trust in the Lord completely; don't ever trust yourself. In everything you do, put God first, and He will direct you and crown your efforts with success" (Proverbs 3:5-6). Oh, by the way--North Carolina won!

BALANCES

Runners need to learn to listen to their bodies, not only to determine what level of training exertion is right for them but also to detect minor problems and correct them before they become injuries.

Three things happen when you run, and two of them are bad. The good one is that you become a more efficient runner. The first bad one is that runners--especially those that run the same slow pace all the time--lose flexibility. Their muscles grow tighter and more susceptible to injury. To prevent this, runners are encouraged to do slow, gentle stretches.

The second bad thing that happens to runners is that they develop strength imbalances. Muscles at the back of the leg overpower those in front, a setup for injury. In addition, the muscles of the upper body lag in strength behind those of the lower body which get all the exercise. Runners are advised to supplement running with exercises that restore strength balances and make fitness more complete.

Do you have enough power and strength to meet your everyday needs? If the answer is no, perhaps the problem lies with the two basic balances to the Christian's life--prayer and Bible study. These can stretch and strengthen our lives with God's power. Wouldn't you like to increase the blessings of the Lord in your life?

OLD CANE POLE

Have you ever gone fishing with an old cane fishing pole? If you have, you know how weak and unstable it is. It can easily be broken by too much weight. Now that's the way Peter was before he met Jesus--easily swayed by circumstances or by people, and he got bent out of shape when somebody crossed him.

Then one day, Jesus came along. And He said to Peter, "Follow me, and I will make you..." (Matthew 4:19). You are Simon now, but I will change you. You shall become Peter, the rock.

In a moment's time, Jesus can give you the miracle of a changed heart and life, but at the same time, a changed life is a "becoming" experience--a change which takes place as you follow Jesus...daily. It's learning how to live by His teachings, how to discipline yourself and bring your life under the authority of God's Word, and how to walk by faith. Jesus takes your weaknesses and like Peter, He makes you...changes you...into a strong, stable person with the courage to face life's problems positively and powerfully.

COACHING TIP

The Bible is like a compass--it always points you in the right direction.

THREE TIMELESS TRUTHS

Some time ago, I read these words of wisdom. No matter what sport you play, these three timeless truths can and will apply (most of all, to the game of life).

(1) FAILURE IS NOT FATAL. Failure should be a teacher to us, not an undertaker. Every kick of failure should kick us forward. If we stumble, we stumble forward. Failure should push us upward to new heights of accomplishment, not pull us down to new depths of despair.

Paul writes to Timothy these words: "...I suffer imprisonment, but the word of God is not imprisoned" (2 Timothy 2:9). Note the word "but." That word "but" is an open door to any failure, any circumstance. (See Romans 8:28).

(2) DELAYS ARE NOT DEADLY. Sometimes, when delays occur, we feel that God has neglected or abandoned us. But delays are the Lord's way of teaching us patience. Why? Because the Lord knows that patience is a daily necessity in our lives. It is not an option; it is a required play in the game of life. (See James 1:3-4).

(3) TRIALS ARE ONLY TEMPORARY. Some of the most peace giving words in the Bible are: "And it came to pass." Problems, pressures, trials and tribulations never come to stay...they come to pass. They are temporary when we realize that our internal resources are greater and stronger than the external trial. It is a true statement: Greater is the power in you than any power on earth. (See 1 John 4:4).

COACHING TIP

A Christian should aim to do the will of God -- nothing more, nothing less, nothing else.

A GREAT PITCHER

One day, a little boy with dreams of becoming a great baseball hitter, like Babe Ruth, couldn't find anyone to play with. So he decided to toss the ball up and hit it for batting practice.

The boy tossed the ball up and swung but missed. Strike one! He threw it up again, swung, and missed. Strike two! He threw the ball up once again, took his best swing at it this time but missed again. Strike three! He hesitated for a minute, thought to himself, and then declared, "Boy, what a great pitcher I am!"

Many of us are like this little boy. We are looking for our special talents, but we haven't quite found them yet. We think they are one thing, but they may be something totally different.

Paul writes, "...to each one of us grace (ability) was given according to the measure of Christ's gift" (Ephesians 4:7). You see, we can't give up on ourselves just because we aren't good at something we have tried. It's important to keep a positive attitude and keep searching until we find the thing that we can do best, the thing which the Lord intended for us to do.

COMING HOME

A man who played baseball when he was a boy remembers one game especially. His father was watching the game, a close one, and when the boy stepped up to bat, he hit the ball hard. He ran around first and second base with the roar of the crowd in his ears, but when he would have held at third, he heard his father shouting above the crowd, "Come on home, boy. Come on home!"

In the years since his father went home to be with the Lord, the son says, "There have been times when the going was a little hard for me, and I have been tempted to do less than my best. But then I hear Dad saying, 'Come on home, boy. Come on home!'"

Jesus said, "I go to prepare a place for you: (John 14:2). The place He is preparing for us is all that the word home connotes--and indescribably more. That in itself should cause us to run with patience the race that is set before us, despite the opposition and obstacles along the way. No matter where we find ourselves along the journey home, His Word encourages us not to falter, but to "come on home."

THE ENCOURAGER

A young man who had played football in high school was trying out for a college team. Within the first few days of practice, he met his coach from the school he formerly attended.

"How's practice going?" the coach asked.

"Not too good," replied the boy. "There are more than two hundred guys out for the team. Many of them are bigger and stronger than I am."

To this the coach responded, "I don't care if there are two hundred guys out for the team and if they are all bigger and stronger than you are. I know you are good enough to make the team. You have what it takes!"

It is a real boost to our confidence when others express a belief in us, and it can encourage us to reach beyond ourselves to attain things we might otherwise not attempt. But we don't need to rely solely on other people to point out our potential. We have God's Word. When we are struggling with self-doubt, we can read a verse like Philippians 4:13, which reminds us we have what it takes: "I can do all things through (Christ) who strengthens me." We have the power of Jesus Christ in us. Even when we are struggling against overwhelming odds, He enables us to become all that God intends us to be.

COACHING TIP

Christianity is not a way of doing certain things but a certain way of doing all things.

MOON WALK

Crossing the finish line first or catching the winning touchdown pass is an exciting experience. But I remember a story about astronaut James Irwin that must have been really exciting too.

It was in 1971, while on the fourth moon walk, as Irwin recalls, "I can't describe to you the thrill of looking out into space and seeing it as only a handful of men have ever seen it. The sun and stars were breathtaking. Then I looked in another direction, and there, hanging like a giant marble, was the earth. I could hardly contain myself.

"I came to a stop, moon dust settling in my boots, and I thought, 'Wow! This is the greatest miracle in the history of the human race. Man is walking on the moon!' Then the Lord spoke to my heart, 'No Jim. It isn't, really. The greatest miracle in the history of mankind is not that man walked on the moon, it's that God walks on the earth and lives in you.'"

As the apostle Paul wrote, "Christ liveth in me" (Galatians 2:20), you and I have experienced the greatest miracle of mankind--God through His Son has set us free from sin and has offered us the privilege of walking in His presence.

SPIRITUAL HEALTH

For an athlete, the three basics are (1) eat right; (2) exercise right; and (3) rest right. With this in mind, let's look at five basics for staying spiritually fit.

1. **Watch what you eat.** We need to take in the truth of God's Word and avoid the kind of input that is spiritually harmful (1 Peter 2:2).

2. **Guard your mouth.** To avoid dental problems it is important to practice oral hygiene. Equally, clean speech avoids spiritual decay (James 3:6; Ephesians 4:29).

3. **Check your hearing and vision.** Look only at what helps you stay on the road of righteousness (Proverbs 4:25). Refuse to listen to gossip, but pay attention to wise counsel (Proverbs 4:1,10).

4. **Control stress.** If you are angry or tense, learn to say no, learn to lean on the Lord, and learn to be patient (Ephesians 4:26; Proverbs 3:5-6; James 5:7,10).

5. **Check your heart.** Be sure you are doing all you can to keep your "heart" strong and pure (Proverbs 4:23; 1 Timothy 1:5).

As athletes keep their bodies fit, so you and I must take preventive steps to maintain spiritual health.

TALENT--REPUTATION--EGO

No matter what sport you play, you need to remember three things: **Talent is God-given, so be thankful. Reputation is human-given, so be humble. Ego is self-given, so be watchful.**

1. Whether we are a coach, athlete or fan, all of us have one or more talents for which we should be thankful to the Living God. All that we have comes from the Lord. He is the Source of all talents, time, and treasures. Without the Lord, we are nothing; with Him, we can do all things (see John 15:5).

2. Reputation is human-given. Therefore, we should be humble because whatever humans give, humans can take away. Reputation is fleeting--only character abides. When we concentrate on building our character, we have no time left to worry about our reputation (see Romans 12:1-2).

3. Ego is self-given, and we should be watchful lest we think more highly of ourselves than we ought to think (see Romans 12:3).

Rejoice thankfully for your God-given talents. Walk humbly in your human-given reputation. Be watchfully cautious of your self-given ego.

COACHING TIP

Never look back unless that's the direction you want to go.

THE GREAT UPSET

One of the greatest race horses of all time was Man O' War. He only lost one race.

When Man O' War would get into his long stride, no horse could keep up. The jockeys of other horses knew that, so they got together before a race and decided to surround Man O' War before he turned on his final burst of speed. Near the finish line they got their horses on all sides of him and cut him off. Man O' War struggled, then finally broke through, but it was too late. He lost by a nose to a horse named Upset.

Man O' War lost because his momentum was hindered. Upset didn't have a chance until that happened.

Have you ever had an "upset" in your life? Everything was going fine, and then suddenly, you found yourself under heavy pressure.

There is a way for you to win under pressure: by keeping your momentum--having faith--looking to the Lord and trusting Him. Often when we look to ourselves for strength, we're discouraged. When we look to others, we're distracted. But when we keep our focus on Jesus, we are never disappointed. Hebrews 12:2 advises, "...fixing our eyes on Jesus, the author and perfecter of faith..."

When your mind is fixed on Jesus, you'll have peace inside, for nothing can upset that which is God-set!

THE "BANNISTER EFFECT"

What is known as the "Bannister effect" shows us how the boundaries of our believing can block us from a desired goal. Up until 1954, no runner had been able to run a mile under 4 minutes. Many tried, but no one could break the 4 minute barrier. Then Roger Bannister managed to do it...falling exhausted across the finish line just a split second under 4 minutes. After that, many runners broke the 4 minute mile. What made the difference? It wasn't that all those runners improved in terms of skill. What appears to be the case is that the belief barrier was broken. Now the runners knew it could be done.

You and I can make a difference in the lives of those around us. Our Lord said, "Let your light shine before men, that they may see your good works, and glorify your Father which is in heaven" (Matthew 5:16). When we use our faith in Jesus to receive answers to prayer for our needs, it can help others to believe for their needs too.

BATTING STANCE

Some years ago, Rick Dempsey was the catcher for the Baltimore Orioles, and Frank Robinson was the batting coach. By Rick's sixth season in the big leagues, he still had no set batting stance. Coach Robinson estimated that Dempsey had tried at least 30 different stances.

"Rick changes even when he's going good," said Robinson. "He's working for perfection. But there's no such thing as a perfect hitter. Every batter makes outs. Even the best, the .300 hitters, fail seven out of ten times."

Failing often makes us feel we need to change our life. Like Rick, we think we need a different stance. But a failure doesn't show us that our entire life is wrong; it shows us one area to keep trying in.

Consistency and persistence are part of a life of faith. The Bible doesn't command us to be successful. Nowhere does God demand that we succeed. He commands us to be faithful.

When you and I believe God and do things with Him, He gives the power to see things through. Jesus said, "(Father), I have finished the work which Thou hast given Me to do" (John 17:4). Paul wrote, "I finished my course, I have kept the faith" (2 Timothy 4:7). Faithfulness is not reached by constantly changing. We find faithfulness in persisting in the areas where we fail. Achievement is the result of continuous effort.

OVERCOMING FAITH

Every runner wants to run faster and further. And you can achieve your goal, as long as you go about doing it the right way. The most common mistake recreational runners make is running too much, too fast, too soon. Improvement is what running is all about, but it must be steady, a gradual process.

Improvement in a Believer's life is the same way. Learning to walk by faith is a process, steady and true. With the burdens we face, it is sometimes hard to think that we could live above them. But we can! 1 John 5:4 says, "This is the victory that overcometh the world, even our faith." Faith is the victory, for faith makes the promise of Jesus real to us.

Romans 10 shows us the process through which faith translates God's power into our daily lives. First, the hearing of faith occurs. Romans 10:17 says, "Faith cometh by hearing and hearing by the word of God." Hearing Scripture (listening to it, reading it, or studying it) opens the ears of our hearts. We hear the Word as though God were speaking directly to us.

Secondly, God's Word settles into our hearts. We receive it, not as a word of our mind, but as a word of faith. God's Word becomes our word. We believe it will help us in our problems.

Finally, we make this word of faith a confession of faith. Romans 10:8 states, "The word is nigh thee, even in thy mouth." The faith in your heart becomes so strong that you want to say it--"I'm saved," or "The Lord is answering my prayer." As you speak the Word you've heard and believed, you release your faith...and your faith brings you the answers you so desperately need.

COACHING TIP

Do what you can, where you are, with what you have.

CONTROLLING CIRCUMSTANCES

He came out of nowhere to win the Boston Marathon with a U.S. record of 2:09.55. During his record run, he stopped to tie his shoelaces. He is Bill Rodgers, who later won the Boston three more times and the New York City Marathon four times.

To a runner, an untied shoe can cost the race. Rodgers took control of his circumstances, knowing it would cost him precious time.

God has placed faith within us to control life's circumstances. When this faith finds a place in our thinking and believing, when we start to act upon the Word of God, then our faith comes forth. God expects us to use our faith. He will not do everything for us; there are some things He requires us to do for ourselves. He works through us to make our prayers realities.

When we are working with the Lord through our faith, we are in control of circumstances instead of being controlled by them. We do not merely accept the things handed to us in life, but we step forward with determination and faith and make the right things happen.

THE STEEL CURTAIN

In 1974, the Pittsburgh Steelers never used the "Stunt 4-3" defense during the regular season. Finally, in the playoffs, it was used first against the Bills. Holding O.J. Simpson to 49 yards gave the Steelers the confidence to use it the following week in the championship game against the Raiders. Pittsburgh held them to 29 yards rushing.

The Super Bowl that followed, against the Minnesota Vikings, was one of devastating rushing shutdowns. Mean Joe Greene, L. C. Greenwood, Jack Lambert and the rest of the Steelers' defense made rushing a bad dream for the Vikes. Despite Chuck Forman and the scrambling of Fran Tarkenton, Minnesota finished with 17 total rushing yards.

Faith in a good defensive plan was the key to the Pittsburgh Steelers' win in Super Bowl IX. No matter what you are facing today, through God your battle can be won. He is able to do "exceeding abundantly above all that we ask or think, according to the POWER that is at work in us" (Ephesians 3:20). Your faith generates that power to overcome. Faith in God is your victory.

THERE'S THE CHURCH

Often when we see a church building we say, "There's the Church." But we can't put the Church within four walls. The Church is the Body of Christ, a living organism made up of people who are born of the Spirit of God (see 1 Corinthians 12:13-31). Christ is not in four walls; He's in hearts. The church building is a place wherein we worship, a place where God is in the midst of His people, but the real Church is in us.

Going to church doesn't make you a Christian, anymore than going into a garage makes you a car. But it does enhance and strengthen your ability to live the way Christ taught us to live.

You can worship the Lord anytime and anywhere, for your relationship with Him is a personal thing. But attending worship with other Christians is a special blessing of strength and help in your Christian walk.

COACHING TIP

Don't pretend to be what you don't intend to be.

THE CARPENTER'S SHOP

One day the tools in a carpenter's shop were arguing among themselves about which of them belonged in the shop. The hammer began to brag about how important it was. But the others said, "We don't need you. You're too noisy. You'll have to leave."

The hammer said, "If I have to leave, so does the plane. It only deals with things on the surface."

"If I have to go," said the plane in dismay, "then so does the nail. It is always getting into things that have nothing to do with it."

The nail was insulted. "Well, if I have to leave, then the ruler must go. It's always measuring others by itself, thinking it's the standard."

Just then, the carpenter walked into the shop. He was the Carpenter of Nazareth. He picked up the tools and started working with them. He was going to build a Church. All the tools looked around and said, "We are all needed. We're all working for the Master."

The Carpenter of Nazareth--Jesus Christ--needs all Christians working together to build His Church. No one can say another member of the Body of Christ is not needed. We're all important in working for the Master.

OF ONE MIND

When a basketball coach took over her team, she had nothing but a string of defeats. She sensed that attitudes of envy and jealousy were undermining the efforts of the team. Each player wanted to be a star. After the coach persuaded them to lay aside their petty feelings and work for the common good, a new spirit began to develop. They started to make personal sacrifices. Hours were spent in practice in order to accomplish the larger goal. The result? They set a record of victories so sensational that all the team members received recognition.

Just as disunity destroys teamwork, the apostle Paul was deeply aware that disunity can seriously damage the church. He counseled the Philippian believers to check for the symptoms of vanity and strife (Philippians 2:3).

His advice is still relevant today. Only by honestly confessing our feelings of resentment and jealousy and by squelching every expression of pride can we hope to be "of one accord, of one mind."

COACHING TIP

In the Lord's eyes, it is a great thing to do a little thing well.

UNFORGETTABLE MOMENT

During the 1982 World Series, a newscaster asked Joe DiMaggio this question: "What was your most unforgettable moment when you played in the World Series?"

Joe, one of the greatest baseball hitters of all time, smiled and replied, "The time I dropped two fly balls on two consecutive pitches."

Now that's just like most of us. We seem to always think about our failures instead of our successes. But the good news is that through Jesus Christ our mistakes can be forgiven...and forgotten. We forget them--not by hiding them in the back of our mind, but by openly bringing them to Jesus and asking Him for forgiveness. Many of us stop there--we let the Lord forgive us, but we don't forget our mistakes.

The key to forgetting our sins is to accept Jesus' forgiveness and then to forgive ourselves as well. The Lord says, "I, even, I am he who blots out your transgressions...(who) remembers your sins no more" (Isaiah 43:25). The Lord promises to forgive and forget our sins--giving us the privilege and power to do the same.

THE DEPTHS OF THE SEA

A young boy had just given his life to Jesus, and he was so excited about it that even in his class at school he would sometimes burst out with "Praise the Lord!" His teacher told him not to disturb the others in class, but the boy said that since he had given his heart to the Lord, many things he read in his textbooks reminded him of what had happened in his life and he just wanted to praise the Lord.

"But you can't bother others in class," his teacher said. "Read your geography book. That should keep you quiet for a while."

But shortly the student was saying "Praise the Lord!" again. His teacher scolded him once again.

"But my geography book," he explained, "says there's a place in the ocean where they haven't found the bottom yet. Praise the Lord, that must be where my sins are!"

Isn't it great to know that when we are forgiven of our sins they are gone forever? (see Micah 7:19). The Bible promises us that the Lord will remember them no more and they can't be held against us. We can live a life free from guilt because, as the prophet Micah said, our sins have been cast "into the depths of the sea."

THE DOG PREACHED A SERMON

Once a stray dog wandered into football practice and the coach threw a rock at it to chase it away. His throw was stronger than he meant it to be. He hit the dog, breaking its leg. Instead of running away, the dog limped up to him and licked his hand. He said, "That day I truly understood the words of Jesus as that dog preached the Sermon on the Mount to me."

In the days of Jesus, the custom was to give a light slap on the face of an enemy to show your dislike for him. It was meant to be more insulting than painful. But Jesus admonished His disciples not to retaliate against those who mistreat them, but to forgive them (see Luke 6:27-28). When He spoke of turning the other cheek, He didn't mean for us to be passive, for some situations do require that we defend ourselves. But He desired that we show a willingness to return good for evil.

Think about this, to return good for good is human, but to return good for evil is Christ-like. The world needs to see a likeness of Jesus in every believer. His love can replace anger with love and grudges with forgiveness as we become living examples of God's Word.

COACHING TIP

God formed us; Sin deformed us; Jesus Christ transforms us.

FOUR THINGS

There are four things that the Lord doesn't know.

1. The Lord doesn't know a sinner that He does not love. From the moment God first looked upon humankind, He has loved us. And His love has never wavered through the ages. In Jeremiah 31:3 God tells us, "I have loved you with an everlasting love."

2. The Lord doesn't know a sin that He does not hate. God hates sin because it destroys the creation that He loves. "The wages of sin is death," Romans 6:23 tells us, and God did not create us for death but for life.

3. The Lord doesn't know a better plan of salvation than the one He offers in His Son, Jesus Christ. He sent His only Son, Jesus, to die on the cross to pay for our sins. Now we don't have to die, but we can have eternal life (see John 3:16).

4. The Lord doesn't know a better time than now to receive His plan. The Bible says, "Now is the accepted time; behold, now is the day of salvation" (2 Corinthians 6:2). His gift of salvation is offered freely to you. You can accept it today by asking Jesus to come live in your heart.

WINNERS EVERY TIME!

In one of the greatest mile duels ever, Marty Liquori defeats Jim Ryun in the first "Dream Mile," a race that lived up to its billing. Held as part of the Martin Luther King International Freedom Games in Philadelphia, Liquori holds off Ryun by inches as both men are timed in 3:54.6.

In God's eyes, a winner is not just the person who receives a trophy, a gold medal, or a blue ribbon. It is anyone who does his or her best and expects God to do His best. It's the person who heeds Ecclesiastes 9:10, "Whatever thy hand findeth to do, do it with thy might," and who confesses Philippians 4:13, "I can do all things through Christ which strengtheneth me." In other words, a winner is one who produces his or her greatest effort and then looks to God as the Source of added strength and ability.

God doesn't require that we win first place or always get top honors. He simply asks that we give our best and then believe that He will give us His best. When we put ourselves wholeheartedly into the challenge before us, we're winners every time!

THE VIKINGS' DISAPPOINTMENTS

There has to be a loser in the Super Bowl. But the Minnesota Vikings have lost the most. In the four Super Bowls during the '70s, the Vikes (1) never had the lead, (2) never scored in the first half and (3) never kicked a successful field goal.

They were defeated by the Chiefs, Dolphins, Steelers and the Raiders. They were outscored, 95 to 34. For this they have suffered persecution.

The Vikings defensive end, Carl Eller, who played in all four defeats admonishes, "Just remember, we were still better than all the other NFC teams. People just remember the winners. They forget how hard it is to get there."

That's like us. We get so disappointed when we want one thing from God, and we receive something entirely different. We fuss or pout or blame the Lord for treating us so badly.

But life's disappointments are often God's set appointments. He appoints things for us in life, things which may disappoint us at first but which, sooner or later, prove to be giant blessings...because God's gifts to us are always good!

COACHING TIP

God loves every one of us as if there were but one of us to love.

HUMAN'S QUESTIONS--GOD'S ANSWERS

These questions are most often asked by those who are wanting answers to their problems from God's Word:

* Am I accountable to God?

"So, then, every one of us shall give account of himself to God" (Romans 14:12).

* Will God punish me for sin?

"For the wages of sin is death" (Romans 6:23).

* Is there hope for me?

"The Lord is...not willing that any should perish, but that all should come to repentance" (2 Peter 3:9).

* How can I be saved?

"Believe on the Lord Jesus Christ, and thou shalt be saved" (Acts 16:31).

* Does God want to save me?

"Christ Jesus came into the world to save sinners" (1 Timothy 1:15).

* Am I saved immediately when I believe?

"He that believeth on the Son hath everlasting life" (John 3:36).

* When can I be saved?

"...now is the accepted time; behold, now is the day of salvation" (2 Corinthians 6:2).

* Can I come just the way I am?

"...him that cometh to me I will in no wise cast out" (John 6:37).

* How should I live after I'm saved?

"...they who live should not henceforth live unto themselves, but unto Him who died for them" (2

Corinthians 5:15).

* What about death and the hereafter?

"I go to prepare a place for you,...that where I am, there ye may be also" (John 14:2-3).

COACHING TIP

Christ believed is salvation received.

WHY DOES GOD ALLOW
SUFFERING AND EVIL?

The Lord created us with the freedom of choice (Genesis 2). This involves the ability to choose right or wrong and the responsibility to live with the consequences.

According to Genesis 3 and Romans 5, Adam and Eve made a decision that had a devastating effect on all of us. Humankind continues to make wrong and bad choices that increase the problem (Romans 1:18-32).

Evil and sin are often the causes of suffering (Job 1,2; 2 Corinthians 12:7).

Suffering is often a warning to us about the problem of sin and our broken relationship with God (Romans 5:12).

Jesus suffered on the cross for our sins (Colossians 1:20-22; 1 John 3:5,8). He offers grace for our present situation (2 Corinthians 12:9).

Personal trials, for a Christian, are to be used to strengthen our faith (1 Peter 1:5-7; James 1:2-4; Romans 5:3-5; Hebrews 12:7-9; John 9:13).

We may not have all the answers concerning suffering and evil, but a God wise enough to create and rule the universe is wise enough to do what is right concerning our personal lives, no matter what the suffering might be.

GOD WANTS YOU TO KNOW...

You are lost and need to be rescued.

   * Unless one is born again, he cannot see the kingdom of God (John 3:3).
   * All have sinned and fall short of the glory of God (Romans 3:23).

You cannot save yourself.

   * Jesus said, "I am the way, the truth, and the life. No one comes to the Father except through Me" (John 14:6).

You must accept His gift of salvation.

   *God so loved the world that He gave His only begotten Son, that whoever believes in Him should not perish but have everlasting life (John 3:16).
   * The wages of sin is death, but the gift of God is eternal life in Christ Jesus our Lord (Romans 6:23).

You can be sure you are saved.

   *I write these things to you who believe in the name of the Son of God so that you may know that you have eternal life (I John 5:13).

ONE STEP AT A TIME

You can't run well on hard surfaces for long without a good pair of running shoes. What should you look for? The most important factor in running shoes is a comfortable fit. There should be about 1/4 inch of room between your longest toe and the end of the shoe. Your toes also need sufficient width to spread out with each stride; don't buy shoes that leave your toes feeling scrunched.

Another important technical point is to look for a well-cushioned midsole with a padded heel. Expect to pay at least $50 for a good pair of running shoes. It will be worth it in the long run.

Good running shoes are the key to finishing the long run. Following Jesus is the key to guiding our steps in the right direction. Psalm 37:23 says, "The steps of a man are established by the Lord." You may not know what tomorrow holds for you...but the Lord knows. He will lead you in the way that is best for you, and He will lead you one step at a time.

As you take the step that God is guiding you toward now, another one will come into view. God will lead you out of the land of sin and doubt into His promised land of righteousness and faith. He will go with you every inch of the way, making the road plain to you--one step at a time.

INSPIRATIONAL PULL

While training for the Olympics, the Russians realized they were just a fraction behind the times of the U.S. runners. In studying the situation, they found that subconsciously their runners had conditioned themselves to run the same speed every time. They didn't have the inspiration of real competition to drive them on.

So their coaches designed some "inspiration." What they did was take ski rope and tie one end around the runners' waists and the other end to the bumper of a truck. They told them they had two choices--run faster or be dragged. Needless to say, most of them where inspired to move faster.

Sometimes you and I need inspiration too, not to move faster for God, but just to keep moving with God. I'm so glad we're tied to the Holy Spirit. The Spirit, rather than dragging us through life like a truck, lovingly and gently encourages us with the Lord's Word. The Spirit reminds us that Jesus is greater than our problems and that we can do all things in Him. With encouragement like this, we don't give up and quit...we're inspired to run until the race is won (see Romans 8:26; 2 Corinthians 12:9).

COACHING TIP

If you aim for nothing, you're sure to hit it.

HAND IN THE GLOVE

Once we become Christians, the Lord expects to reach others through us. He knows our limitations; therefore, He doesn't want us to minister to others in our own strength--but in His.

Let me give you an example. Suppose you were to take a baseball glove and place it in center field. Then you said to the glove, "Glove, catch the ball." Naturally you wouldn't expect the glove to catch the ball because the glove lacks life. It lacks the power. But suppose you put your hand in the glove and then said, "Glove, catch the ball." Your hand inside the glove would enable it to have a part in catching the ball.

This is a graphic illustration of how the Holy Spirit works in our lives. John 14:17 says, "For he dwelleth with you, and shall be in you." We are the glove, and the Holy Spirit is the hand of the Lord working in and through us. How exciting and fruitful our life becomes when we yield control of it to Jesus!

THREE LOADS

An engineering professor was explaining to her class the complexities involved in bridge building. "When we build a bridge," she said, "we figure on three loads the bridge will bear--the dead load, the live load, and the wind load. The dead load is the weight of the bridge itself. The live load is the weight of the traffic the bridge will bear. The wind load is the pressure of the wind on the superstructure."

Isn't this a parable of life? Life's dead load is concerned with the managing of oneself. The live load is the responsibilities we carry daily. And a simple definition of the wind load would be life's tougher situations that take their toll in our lives.

The Lord has given us the Holy Spirit to enable us to stand up to the pressures of everyday living. When a situation arises that makes us want to fall down, the Holy Spirit within us strengthens and upholds us. When we feel we will collapse, the Spirit equalizes the pressure of stress on us.

Paul writes, "you...be strengthened with power through His Spirit in the inner man" (Ephesians 3:16). It is through the power of the Spirit that Jesus triumphed, and when we use this power, we, too, are able to withstand life's destructive forces.

COACHING TIP

The Lord requires faithfulness; the Lord rewards with fruitfulness.

DOING OUR PART

At a high school track meet, one runner crossed the finish line just ahead of his closest competitor. A bystander noticed the lips of the winner moving during the last two laps. Wondering what the boy was saying, he asked him about it. "I was praying," the runner replied. Pointing to his feet, he said, "I was saying, 'You pick 'em up, Lord, and I'll put 'em down.'" That athlete prayed for the Lord's help, but he also did what he could to answer his prayer himself.

Mark records these words of Jesus, "What things soever ye desire, when ye pray, believe that ye receive them, and ye shall have them" (Mark 11:24). Often our prayer time is spent, not in actual prayer, but in worrying on our knees. After sharing with the Lord just how impossible our situation is, we get up just as distressed as before. Sometimes, telling our problems to the Lord does give a certain sense of relief, but temporary relief isn't the main purpose of prayer. The main purpose is to change the situation causing the trouble.

When you want to see something done, take it to the Lord for help, trusting that He will undertake the problem. No situation is impossible for Him to handle. With an awareness of His power and concern, you can leave each problem in His hands as you go on your way believing and rejoicing, with troubles lifted, confident that the solution to your problems is on the way.

A DEAD DUCK

A group of men were duck hunting when one of them began to boast of his marksmanship. Taking careful aim on a lone duck, he said to the others, "Watch this!"

He fired, but the bird flew on.

"My friends," he spoke with amazement, "you are now witnessing a miracle. There flies a dead duck."

This humorous story makes a point about faith. The Lord wants us to believe that our prayers are answered even when we don't see the answer right away. This is faith: "The assurance of things hoped for, the conviction of things not seen" (Hebrews 11:1).

If we pray for something in God's will, we can believe without a doubt that He will answer. Even if we can't see the results immediately, we are to rest assured that the Lord is faithfully working for our good. We can stand on the promise that: "If we ask anything according to his will he hears us in whatever we ask, we know that we have obtained the requests made of him" (1 John 5:14-15).

COACHING TIP

Kindness is the vocabulary the deaf can hear and the blind can see.

ANSWER TO RIDICULE

Nehemiah was a Jew taken captive to Persia during the reign of King Artaxeres. He was the king's cupbearer when some of the Jews arrived from Jerusalem and told of the desperate conditions and hardship that was there. Nehemiah asked the king if he could return to Jerusalem to help rebuild the walls of the city. Permission was granted.

When Nehemiah's enemies heard of his plans, they laughed at him. They prophesied: "If even a fox walked along the top of their wall, it would collapse!" (Nehemiah 4:3). Nehemiah didn't attempt to answer them. Instead he prayed: "Hear us, O Lord God, for we are being mocked. May their scoffing fall back upon their own heads" (Nehemiah 4:4).

No logical argument will keep us from malicious ridicule. The best solution is to take those who criticize us to the Lord and then devote ourselves to completing our task. When we do this, we will be able to claim victory over our enemies in the way Nehemiah did. He said, "The wall was finally finished...When our enemies...heard about it, they were frightened and humiliated, and they realized that the work had been done with the help of our God" (Nehemiah 6:15-16).

MANNER OF PRAYER

Many of us often recite the Lord's Prayer exactly as Jesus gave it to us. That's good to do, but it's even better to take the spirit of what He said and use it as the basis for all our prayers. Jesus said, "Pray in this manner" (Matthew 6:9). We are to build our prayers on the foundation of these truths found in the Lord's Prayer.

* **God is our Source.** Our prayers are to be directed to the Father and our expectations directed from Him.

* **God's riches in glory are ours.** We should pray for His supply in heaven to come to us here on earth.

* **God is in every moment of our existence.** We can daily ask Him to meet our needs.

* **God is merciful.** When we confess our sins, He will forgive us as we have forgiven others.

* **God won't leave us when times get tough**. He is there to deliver us when we call.

* **God's power triumphs over evil's power.** We can pray with confidence, knowing the Lord can take care of us, no matter how great our problem is.

When we pray in the manner that Jesus taught us, we're praying in a manner that brings results. He will be everything we need Him to be and do everything we need Him to do.

PRAYER AND PERSEVERENCE

Karen Phelps, a distance runner, wrote recently, "On this particular day, I didn't feel like running at all. But I made myself because running is a sport you have to practice every day. I wanted to win races, so I had a set plan for training:

1. Run daily, even if you don't feel like it.

2. Run daily, even if you sometimes have to skip fun and pleasure.

3. Run daily, even in bad weather--even if people think you're weird.

4. Run daily, even when it gives you aches and pains and you feel like quitting.

5. Run daily, even if you don't feel it's doing you any good.

"Sometimes you may not feel like practicing, or doing something else that needs your attention, but if you're in training you'll do it."

Growing in the faith requires perseverence in training, too. Try changing the "run daily" part of the five-step plan above to "pray daily." Set aside a few minutes every day specifically for prayer. Pray for your friends and family and for others who are in need. Also pray for God to be a very real presence in your life.

Matthew 24:13 says, "but the one who endures to the end, he shall be saved." You'll be amazed at how a daily prayer can help you focus on the important things in life.

COACHING TIP

The Christian finds safety not in the absence of danger but in the presence of the Lord.

DO YOU KNOW GOD?

Do you know God personally? Do you talk to Him? Is He your friend? A lot of people know about God, but they've never had any firsthand knowledge of Him. They don't really know Him as a Person.

So the question is, how do you get personally acquainted with God? First of all, you ask someone who already knows Him to introduce you. Jesus is the One who can introduce you to God because He is the One who already knows Him.

So if you want to know God, start with Jesus. Get acquainted with Him first. Read about His life in the first four books of the New Testament - Matthew, Mark, Luke, and John. Talk to Jesus Himself. Open up and tell Him everything about yourself, even the worst things, and ask Him to forgive you for them. Turn around--turn from sin to God. Commit your life to Him and press on to know Him better.

When you get to know Jesus as a person, you will get to know God as person. Jesus said, "If you really (know) me, you (will) know my Father as well" (John 14:7).

A CHRISTIAN IS...

There are three C's that describe a Christian, and they are easy to remember. First, a Christian is a person of CONVICTION. We believe that Jesus is the Messiah, the Savior of the world. Only the Spirit of God can convince us that Jesus Christ is who He claimed to be--the Son of the living and eternal God.

Secondly, a Christian is a person who has COMMITTED his or her life to Jesus' Lordship. There is always a cost involved with this commitment, but it is always worth the cost.

Finally, a Christian is a person whose CONDUCT gives evidence of his or her conviction and commitment. People will know a Christian by his or her behavior. When we live a godly life, others will see Jesus in us. And that's what being a Christian is all about.

HOW TO BE SAVED

There is no special formula to follow in order to be saved, but there are certain things you must do.

One: What you must know.
* That you are a sinner who is hopelessly lost and under the sentence of death. Spiritual death is everlasting separation from the Lord in Hell (see Romans 3:23; 6:23; John 3:18-19; Matthew 25:41,46).
* That you cannot save yourself by any effort of your own (Ephesians 2:8-9).
* That Jesus Christ, God's Son, died on the cross and rose from the dead to pay the penalty for your sins (Romans 5:8; I Peter 2:24; I Corinthians 15:3-4).

Two: What you must do.
* Admit to God that you have sinned and deserve the penalty of death (Romans 3:23).
* Accept Jesus Christ as your personal Savior (John 1:12).
* Acknowledge Jesus Christ as Lord and Savior by confessing with your mouth (Romans 10:9-10).

Three: What God will do.
* Save you (Romans 10:13).
* Forgive you of your sins (Ephesians 1:7).
* Give you eternal life (John 10:28).

Do you want to be saved? If so, pray the following

prayer (or in your own words): Dear Lord Jesus, I have sinned against You and deserve the penalty of death. I believe You died in my place for all my sins. I accept You now into my life as my Savior and my Lord, and I commit my life to You. Amen.

If you have received Jesus as your Savior and Lord, tell someone.

COACHING TIP

When you bend your knees to pray, the Lord bends His ear to listen.

PACE TRAINING

Pace training develops your ability to maintain a fast, cruising speed that is close to your race pace. The idea is to practice a pace you can sustain and control for the duration of your target event. It should be a moderate to somewhat hard effort that is manageable without duress. It is a consistent high-end aerobic effort where you feel in control...your breathing, your movements, your effort...everything is in equilibrium.

To maintain this steady state, you need to slow down on the uphills and speed up on the downhills. The objective is to keep your energy output just below the "red-line."

You'll develop your sense of pace more quickly by sticking to gentle terrain. For running, 3 to 6 mile pace runs are ideal, preferably on the same course so you can compare times and chart your improvement.

Here are some important things all of us should remember for our spiritual pacing.

* Remember to start your day with prayer. Go to the Lord and ask Him to guide you through the day, to help you live unselfishly, abundantly, and victoriously.

* Remember to carry a smile with you. A friendly smile might be the greatest gift you can give to someone who looks to you for inspiration, courage, and/or comfort.

* Remember to give out kindness along the way. Everyone you meet today will be fighting some

kind of personal battle, and your kindness can help him or her to "keep on keeping on."

* Remember to be grateful and to express your gratitude spontaneously and frequently. A sincere "thank you" will give pleasure to others...and bring joy to you!

SUPERSTITIONS

Athletes are often superstitious. They wear a certain hat or t-shirt, maybe even a religious medal, in the belief that the object will bring good luck. We've all heard of knocking on wood after telling others about something that seems almost too good to last. Even Winston Churchill, who was highly educated, once remarked to the House of Commons, "I rarely like to be any considerable distance from a piece of wood." And following that statement, he tapped the nearby table.

There are numerous theories about how this superstition started. Some say it originated from the old game of "wood tag" in which a player who is able to touch wood is safe from capture. Others think its beginning is associated with the cross on which Jesus died. Regardless of how it started, it is only a superstition like crossing your fingers, dodging black cats, and being careful not to open an umbrella indoors.

We never need to yield our mind to any form of superstition. In fact, God commands us, "Have no other gods before me" (Exodus 20:3), and superstition is really nothing more than idolatry. God is the only real answer to all our fears. So, whenever you tell others about something good that has happened in your life, why knock on wood? Instead, give God the credit and praise Him for His presence in your life.

COACHING TIP

When we are good to others, we are good to ourselves.

THE HYMN-SINGER

The night after Orel Hershiser pitched the final game in the '88 World Series to beat the Oakland Athletics, he was a guest on "The Tonight Show." Johnny Carson asked about singing to himself in the dugout, and the audience wanted him to sing his song.

Knowing there was no way out, Hershiser said, "Well, the one I can remember singing the most was just a praise hymn. As I sat on the bench I would sing:

"Praise God from whom all blessings flow.
Praise Him all creatures here below.
Praise Him above ye heavenly host.
Praise Father, Son, and Holy Ghost.
Amen."

Orel describes the audience as deathly quiet. Sometimes people who do not know Jesus Christ as their personal Savior do not understand why Christians are always singing and praising the Lord. For those who don't have a song of praise, it is just noise. They haven't experienced the joy of the Lord and the fullness of the Spirit of God that brings praise bubbling up from within.

But when a person receives salvation and makes Jesus the Lord of his or her life, then that person understands. And the noise isn't bothersome anymore. It becomes a joyful noise.

THE PERFECT EXAMPLE

After a positive drug test at the 1988 Olympics in Seoul, Canadian Ben Johnson was stripped of his gold medal and it was awarded to Carl Lewis. The IAAF gave Johnson, because of his compromise, a two-suspension.

Suppose everybody did it? Suppose everybody did what you do; would the world be better or not as good? Are your standards of conduct so high that you want others to copy them?

Suppose everybody talked as you do. Would there be more or less harmony among people? Do you guard your words so carefully that you would be willing to have everyone talk as you do?

Suppose everybody thought as you do. Would Christianity be a stronger force in the world today? Are your thoughts free of envy, hatred, and fear, worthy to serve as models for others?

Suppose everybody had the faith you have. Would the kingdom of God be nearer, more real, throughout the world? Is your faith strong enough, firm enough, to inspire others to move mountains of doubt?

Of course, only One is worthy of serving as the perfect example: Jesus Christ. Suppose everybody followed His example. Wouldn't this be a perfect world?

BROADWAY JOE'S WHITE SHOES

With his long hair, contagious smile and, of course, his white shoes, Joe Namath made Super Bowl III memorable by "guaranteeing" his team's win. The Colts were a 17-point favorite but Namath and the Jets won, proving that the AFL's time had come. For his leadership Joe was named MVP.

Everyone exerts an influence. It may be positive or negative. The kind of life we live, the type of service we render, the quality of attitude we have, all determine the depth and breadth of our influence.

If we habitually practice selfishness, our influence will be shallow. If we give ourselves generously for the benefit of others, our influence will be deep and lasting. If our love is Christlike in its scope, Godlike in its depth, and childlike in its trust, our positive influence will be everlasting.

COACHING TIP

Love reduces friction to a fraction.

29 YEARS A COWBOY

For 29 years, Dallas fans saw Tom Landry standing on the sidelines. He'd become a legend. When he began with the Cowboys, he was the youngest head coach in the NFL. When he finished, he was the oldest.

Landry guided his Cowboys to two Super Bowl wins, 1972 against Miami and 1978 against Denver. They lost both SB's with Pittsburgh (1976 and 1979), and they lost their first attempt, in 1971, against the Colts.

As Coach Landry guided the Cowboys to many victories, so our Lord guides us. Jesus Christ knows every dark valley we face, every mountain we climb, every step we take. And He promises to lead and guide us.

You don't have to fear where life will take you today. You can put your trust in Jesus who said, "I am with you always, even to the end of the world" (Matthew 28:20).

TEN FUTURE MISSIONARIES

Ten future missionaries heard God's call divine
One was married wrongly, and that left only nine
Nine future missionaries, they could hardly wait
Mother needed one, and that left only eight
Eight future missionaries bound for God and heaven
One got to making money, and that left only seven
Seven future missionaries, if only each one sticks
One lost out completely, and that left only six
Six future missionaries for God alive
One preferred the wildlife, and that left only five
Five future missionaries bound for eternity
Two got tired of waiting, and that left only three
Three future missionaries, for the need so few
One the Church rejected, and that left only two
Two future missionaries, a daughter and a son
One developed ulcers, and that left only one
One future missionary, thank God for him
He refused to let the vision dim
Body, soul, and spirit, to God he did yield
Now for years he's been on the mission field
God of Heaven rejoices, "Blessed child of Mine.
You've done my will, but what about the nine?"

Author unknown

COACHING TIP

Knowing that the Lord sees us brings both conviction and confidence.

GOD'S BATTLE

The Word of God likens the Christian life to a wrestling match. Paul tells us, "We wrestle not against flesh and blood but against principalities... powers...rulers of the darkness of this world...spiritual wickedness in high places" (Ephesians 6:12). We wrestle! Two powers are constantly trying to divide our lives. The Lord is reaching toward us with His love and presence. At the same time, evil is grabbing at us with a hand of fear, doubt and sin.

As long as we are in this life, we are right in the middle of this spiritual wrestling match. And the victory goes to the strongest.

We alone are no match for evil, but we are mighty through the Lord. That's why we must be armed with God's armor, using the spiritual weapons that He gave us to use. We can never win this match relying upon our own intellect or strength. We must rely upon the only power that is greater than evil's...the resurrection power of Jesus and His Holy Spirit who is working within us in the battle. It is through this power that we will win!

RUNNING TO WIN

In the 1972 Summer Olympics, Jim Ryun was expected to reach the peak of his career as a world class miler. He had trained hard for the 1,500 meter run and was favored for the gold medal.

But in the preliminaries, another runner bumped hard into Ryun, staggering him. He stumbled and fell. Once down, there was no way for Ryun to win--not even a chance for him to get into the medal race. Yet Ryun didn't stay down on the track. Scrambling to his feet, he finished the race.

The apostle Paul compares the Christian life to running a race. He said, "Run in such a way that you may win" (1 Corinthians 9:24). The writer to the Hebrews wrote, "...let us run with endurance the race that is set before us..." (Hebrews 12:1). Endurance, not speed, is the goal in the human race, and everyone can be a winner. Like Jim Ryun, even the most dedicated of us can stumble in life's race. But by having an attitude of endurance, an "I-can-make-it!" determination, you and I can get back up and into the race.

Ecclesiastes 9:11 says, "...the race is not to the swift..." speed is essential to competitive running, endurance is the objective in the Christian race.

GREATER IS HE IN ME

Some time ago, I read a story of a prize fighter who traveled with the circus during the 1920's. He was a small man, but on most occasions, he had been known to beat men twice his size. Naturally, he drew large crowds in the small towns the circus played.

When asked how he could take on bigger and stronger men, he would always reply, "It's not the size of the dog in the fight that's important. It's the size of the fight in the dog."

Have you ever looked at your problems and said, "They're too big for me to handle?" Listen, even if you think the situation you're in is big enough to knock you out, you can lick it. Just like that circus fighter, it's what's in you that really counts.

That "what" is really a "who"--Jesus Christ. He is powerful enough to take on any problem life hits you with and bring you through it with victory! When you think your problems are too big to handle in your own strength, remember the encouraging words of the apostle John, "Greater is He that is in you, than he that is in the world" (1 John 4:4).

COACHING TIP

Keep out of your life all that would crowd Jesus out of your heart.

LIFTING WEIGHTS

A little boy was trying to lift his daddy's barbells. He really tried hard, but he didn't have the strength to lift the heavy weights. His father, who was watching, asked, "Son, are you using all your strength?"

"I'm really trying to," said the boy.

"Try again," his father said, "and this time use all the strength you have."

The little boy struggled with all his might but couldn't budge the weights. "It's no use," he said, "I can't do it."

"You're still not using all your strength," his father told him.

"What do you mean?" the son asked.

"You haven't asked me to help you," the father replied.

How often we struggle with problems and troubles that frustrate us and threaten to defeat us when all the time Father is standing by, just waiting for us to ask Him for His help! Philippians 4:13 tells us: "I can do all things through Him who strengthens me." The Lord's strength becomes our strength when we turn our problems and troubles over to Him.

POWERFUL WORDS

The following words can give an athlete the leading edge:

GOD IS!

I AM!

WITH HIM, I CAN!

GOD IS!

He is our "refuge and strength, a very present help in time of trouble" (see Psalm 46:1). He is our joy in the present; our hope for the future; the God of the now, the Master of this moment.

I AM! I am an adopted child of God and that makes me royalty. I am important, I am loved, I am needed, I am strong and capable of overcoming any adversity that comes my way (Romans 8:14-15, 28).

WITH HIM! This is the key to real living. Without Him, I am nothing; with Him, I am everything. Without Him, I am helpless; with Him, I can do all things (see Philippians 4:13). Without Him, everything is impossible; with Him, all things are possible (see Mark 9:23).

I CAN! The two most common words used are "I can't," but the two most powerful words are "I can." I can because God is. I can because I am. I can because I am with Him. And my confidence in Him is the foundation, the beginning of a healthy and whole self-confidence.

COACHING TIP

Coming together as a team is a beginning; keeping together as a team is progress; working together as a team is success.

LONG-DISTANCE RUNNING

The Bible describes life as a race. We are told in Hebrews 12 to run this race with patience or endurance.

Here is what happens to a runner's body in a distance race. When the body begins to overheat, sweat glands release liquid to cool it. When it begins to run low on sugar, which is fuel for the muscles, a hormone from the pancreas tells the liver to release stored sugar into the bloodstream. As the legs and heart need more oxygen, the brain signals the heart to beat faster. Blood flow to the internal organs and the upper body is shut down by 80 percent so that more blood gets to the legs and heart. Deep breathing brings in more air. Blood vessels in the legs dilate 400 percent to accommodate the increased flow of blood. All of this enables a person to run long distances.

Just as the Lord has built into the body the capacity to keep running, so too He sustains us spiritually in the race of life. Isaiah declared that when we wait on the Lord, He will renew our strength, and we will run and not grow tired (Isaiah 40:31).

GOD'S CHAMPIONS

Jesse Owens, hailed as the most famous Olympic hero, died in 1980 at the age of 65. He did more than win four gold medals in the Berlin Games of 1936. Jesse won despite direct racial criticism from Adolf Hitler.

Hitler had mocked Jesse and his teammates, calling them "America's black auxiliaries." But Owens refused to be intimidated by the Fuhrer's words and his "master race" philosophy. He persevered and became an Olympic world champion sprinter and long-jumper.

Jesse Owens reminds us of many heros in the Bible. Moses was mocked and scorned by Pharaoh, but he delivered more than a million Israelites from Egyptian bondage. Noah was ridiculed by the immoral people of his day, but he built an ark which safely carried him and his family through the great flood that destroyed all living things. Although others wanted them to fail, each of these men persevered and accomplished what the Lord wanted them to do.

The apostle Paul said, "If God is for us, who is against us?" (Romans 8:31). When we determine to persevere in our task, then no one and nothing can keep us from accomplishing God's will.

PRESS ON

In the summer of '84, in Los Angeles, Joan Benoit (now Samuelson) won the first Olympic Marathon for women. She triumphed by an astounding 86 seconds over Grete Waitz in the historic race. Benoit has become the greatest American marathoner in history, setting a marathon world record, winning two Boston Marathons and one Chicago.

For most marathoners the temptation to give up and quit happens between the seventeenth and twentieth mile. They call it the "wall." So great is the temptation to quit, that with every step, your body is screaming "Stop!" In the Christian life, there are "walls." Paul wrote the Philippians declaring, "I press on toward the goal to win the prize for which God has called me" (chapter 3:14).

Where is God leading you? Do the goals you have set seem unreachable? Has time passed, and you've seen no evidence of making any progress toward them? Then the words of Paul remind us that we can reach our goals, in spite of the walls, if we don't give up.

COACHING TIP

Time misspent is not lived but lost.

IS ANYBODY OUT THERE?

The coach of a little league baseball team told his players to talk to one another and yell to each other on the field. He knew that the pitcher could sometimes feel alone or tense and needed their encouragement.

One day, the team was playing a tough game. In the bottom of the ninth inning, they were ahead by one run, with the bases loaded and two outs. Their pitcher faced the batter with a full count, two strikes and three balls. The stands were quiet. Suddenly the coach yelled from the dugout, "Is anybody out there?"

The players came alive and began to chatter. Feeling they were backing him up, the pitcher rocketed the ball past the plate. It was all over. He had thrown a strike, and won the game.

Do you know someone who is in the midst of a tough situation? If they're like most of us, they probably feel they're facing the pressure all alone. Going through their heart and mind are these questions, "Does anyone care? Is anybody out there?" You can be the one to respond, to let them know the Lord loves them. Through a word of encouragement, you can give them the inspiration they need to keep going strong (see Hebrews 3:13; Galatians 6:7).

COMMUNICATION SKILLS

Coaches are taught that in trying to communicate their point to their team, only 7 percent of what's heard depends on the actual words used. Another 38 percent of what gets their point across is based on the way it is said. The coach's body language and inflection or the expression in his or her voice determines how the point is heard. Then, 55 percent of a coach's effective communication depends on whether he or she is trusted by the team.

It's the same in communicating and reaching others for Christ. It isn't enough to use the right words. What's important is that we use the right words with the right tone of voice, after establishing a relationship of trust. A sign in front of a church said: "People don't care how much you know until they know how much you care!"

Jesus challenges us with these words, "By this all men will know that you are My disciples, if you have love for one another" (John 13:35). When you share your love for others, not only with words but also with actions, you speak a language they can understand. The language of Jesus--love.

COACHING TIP

Think you can--think you can't--either way you're right.

CLIMBING THE MOUNTAIN

A mountain climbing instructor took his class of novice climbers on their first climb. The mountain was not too high and three of the big hefty fellows made it to the top in a few hours. But some of the climbers made it only halfway and were exhausted. Others made it only a few hundred feet, for they spent most of their time struggling to get out of crevices they had fallen in.

When the climbers regrouped at the end of the day, the instructor said, "Tomorrow I'm going to share with the group the secret of mountain climbing. I'll show you how all of you can make it to the top." The next day, he took the class to the same mountain. He tied them all together with a rope and they began to work together. Those who were strong helped the weak. When some fell down, others helped them up. By the end of the day, all the climbers made it to the top.

The Lord never intended for us to climb trouble (mountains) alone. He made us a unified body so we can help one another through life's tough places. Solomon shares this bit of wisdom: "Two are better than one because they have a good return for their labor. For if either of them falls, the one will lift up his companion. But woe to the one who falls when there is not another to lift him up" (Ecclesiastes 4:9-10).

When the body of believers walk together, work together, worship together, no problem is so great that it can't be overcome.

TURN THE FOCUS TO JESUS

The Washington Redskins hardly seemed super a year before they met the Miami Dolphins in the Super Bowl in 1983. Instead, they were plagued by adversity. They started the 1981 season with a 0-5 record, and many players were sidelined with injuries. They were ranked last out of 28 teams and hadn't won a world championship in 40 years.

The Skins began the '82 season with a new strategy. Under the leadership of Head Coach Joe Gibbs and Chaplain Jim Brenn, the team started applying Bible principles to football, and as one sports writer said, "This season blossomed into the most blessed of all its 46 years."

Washington finished the season with a winning record and entered the playoffs. After a win over the Cowboys, the entire team knelt in the locker room, joined hands, and prayed the Lord's Prayer together. They went on to defeat Miami 27-17 and now each team member has a Super Bowl ring that says he's a champion.

Both adversity and triumph tend to focus attention on us. What great opportunities they are for us to turn the focus to Jesus and give Him the glory!

SEVEN STEPS OUT OF FEAR

There are only two fears with which human beings are born, according to psychologists--the fear of loud noises and the fear of falling. All other fears are learned.

Let's look at the steps out of fear.

First, **if you have a fear, don't be afraid to admit it.** If you conceal a fear, it will be driven into the subconscious, and there it will work havoc. Bring it up and out and look at it.

Second, **give up all justification for your fears.** Fears are disruptive; therefore, they cannot be right. God wills wholeness.

Third, **fix in your mind the idea that to be afraid is foolishness.** These are the words of Jesus, "How foolish you are, and how slow of heart to believe" (Luke 24:25). Faith, not fear, should characterize all your thinking and acting.

Fourth, **since fears are foolish, surrender them to the Lord.** If you surrender your fears to God, then He has them, not you. This surrendering is important--you are not struggling to overcome them; you and God are working it out together. Your eyes are now on the Lord and not on yourself and your fears. Focusing on God creates faith; focusing on yourself and your fear creates more fear.

Fifth, **keep repeating to yourself this verse: "There is no fear in love. But perfect love drives out fear"** (1 John 4:18). This verse is important, for if there is "no fear in love," then the obvious thing for you to do is to love, to love everybody. Fear can come only where love is not. Where love is, fear is not. The more loving you become, the more love you get back.

Sixth, **meet the fears of life one day at a time.** God has arranged for life to come to us in manageable portions--one day at a time. Remember this bit of wisdom:

Life by the yard is hard
But life by the inch is a cinch.

Finally, **the seventh step out of fear is accepting the Holy Spirit within you as the source of your peace and power.** God, the Holy Spirit, moves in and takes over where fears have reigned. He is there--in control. In a hotel room was a sign on the door: "Rest assured. Bolt your door." But suppose you can't bolt your doors against fears--they are within--then what? You cannot "rest assured" unless the rest is within. The Spirit within is adequate for anything and everything around you today.

COACHING TIP

A good leader is one who knows the way and shows the way.

LIVING FLAMES

Tourists stood in Olympic Stadium in Athens, Greece, as their guide explained how the Olympic Games began there. "A torch is lighted in Olympia," he said. "A runner takes that torch and runs all the way to this stadium. Here the flame from the torch is applied to another one, and another runner takes it and starts with it to the ship that is to carry the Greek team overseas where the games are to be played. That flame is never allowed to go out until the games are over and the winners announced!"

Jesus Christ lit the flame of Christianity. In the land of Abraham, King David, and the Prophets, He applied the flame of His conquering Spirit to the lives of 12 other men. Soon the 12 flames became 120. Before long the 120 became 3,000. The 3,000 became 5,000. And the multiplication kept on until His enemies declared, "All Jerusalem is set aflame with this doctrine!"

Jesus said, "You are the light of the world" (Matthew 5:14). You and I are His torchbearers and that flame must never go out until "the game is over and the winners announced."

I EXPECT GOD WILL

"Do you expect to make an impression on the heathen?" the ship captain asked a missionary who was on his way to China. "No, but I expect God will," was his confident reply.

When the Lord spoke to Moses from the burning bush, He directed him to return to Egypt and demand the liberation of the Jews. In response, Moses pointed out his weaknesses and the reasons why it would be impossible for him to accomplish what God had asked. But the Lord supported His instructions with this promise: "Certainly I will be with thee" (Exodus 3:12). On his own, Moses was unable to convince the Pharaoh to let God's people go, but the power of the Lord convinced him.

The Lord knows about your weaknesses, your faults, your failures-- and your potentialities. But when you yield your life to the leadership of the Lord, He can and will work through you.

COACHING TIP

The conversion of a soul is the miracle of a moment; the growth of a saint is the work of a lifetime.

ILLUMINATED LIFE

Survivors from a shipwreck had been adrift for some time when they spotted a ship approaching. To their dismay, however, the ship sailed past them. They yelled for help but their voices couldn't be heard. Then, to their surprise, the ship changed course and headed in their direction.

"How did you know we were here?" one of the rescued asked.

"We saw your illuminated life preservers," the captain replied.

Jesus said, "Ye are the light of the world. A city that is set on a hill cannot be hid. Neither do men light a candle, and put it under a bushel but on a candlestick, and it giveth light unto all that are in the house" (Matthew 5:14-15).

Although you may not always be aware of it, the power of the Lord is illuminating your life all the time. You may think the people around you are unaware of the light of God's presence in your life. But like a city set on a hill, your light shines forth as a testimony to the Lord's power. And in times of distress, people will be drawn to you for help. Then the Lord can use you to minister to them in their time of need.

COACHING TIP

The more difficult the obstacle, the stronger a person becomes when he hurdles it.